the Carnival, the Life

ALSO BY DAVID ALLAN EVANS

POETRY
This Water, These Rocks (2009)
After the Swan Dive (chapbook, 2008)
Each Day You're Gone (chapbook, 2008)
Images of Place: Paintings and Poems (with Gary Steinley, 2007)
Decent Dangers (2000)
Hanging Out with the Crows (1991)
Real and False Alarms (1985)
Train Windows (1976)
New Voices in American Poetry (editor, 1973)

PROSE
Cultural Meetings: American Writers, Scholars and Artists in China
(co-editor with Jan Evans and Zhang Ziqing, 2003)
Double Happiness: Two Lives in China (with Jan Evans, 1995)
Remembering the Soos (memoir, 1986)

the Carnival, the Life

Poems by

David Allan Evans

SETTLEMENT HOUSE

Library of Congress
Control Number 2013933856
Evans, David Allan
The carnival, the life
ISBN: 978-0-9859468-1-4

First Edition

Manufactured in the United States of America
Cover design by Dale Rimmer
Typesetting/composition by Jocelyn Wascher

SETTLEMENT HOUSE
www.settlementhouse.us

2200 Wilson Blvd., Suite 102 #184
Arlington, VA 22201-3324

ACKNOWLEGEMENTS

Acknowledgments are due to the editors of the following presses, magazines, and anthologies in whose pages the poems in this book first appeared:

Aethlon: The Journal of Sport Literature: "On an Old Black and White Photograph"

The Briar Cliff Review: "Pelicans on Lake Oakwood"

Common Ground Review: "Watching Bull Riders"

Connotation Press: "Protean" (originally called "Red Fox"), "At Crystal Lake," "Primal Winter," "Maya"

Lady Jane's Miscellany: "The Ascent of Squirrels" (originally called "The Evolution of Squirrels"), "Gymnast in Serious Condition after Fall"

Little Balkans Review: "The Details"

Paddlefish: "Youth," "What Comes Back"

Platte Valley Review: "Winter Dyad"

Seems: "Lilies"

South Dakota Review: "Cartoon Universals," "Sixty Years Later I Notice Inside a Flock of Blackbirds"

Spillway: "The Writer"

Water-Stone Review: "Waking Up at Four A.M."

•

The third section of the book previously appeared as a chapbook, *Each Day You're Gone*, published by Red Dragonfly Press.

The poems "Mortal Leaps" and "Turning 70" first appeared in *A Harvest of Words: Contemporary South Dakota Poetry*, edited by Patrick Hicks.

The poem "Dyadic" is re-printed in the anthology *Perfect Dragonfly* edited by Scott King.

Contents

THREE

FOUR

for Jan

ONE

*One does not meet oneself until one catches
the reflection from an eye other than human.*

—Loren Eiseley

Pelicans On Lake Oakwood

All morning they soared on thermals,
   silent as gliders,
      and having traded one blue
         world for another, they've been

paddling around all afternoon—
   white ships with breastbones as
      prows, their wings
         oar locked.

For scooping up fish, and for
   vigilance, a dozen yellow nets and
      two dozen eyes are better than
         one net and two eyes;

so they hang with a crowd.
   Without a teacher, a calendar
      or a clock, they move among
         reeds and willows, or in

open water—eating, contending, mating.
   Always free to go, owned by
      no one and owning nothing,
         any minute they may lift

off with an awkward grace back to
   the other world they're at home in,
      yielding their whiteness to
         the whiteness of clouds.

Waking Up At Four A.M.

I reach back and grab a cool metal bar
at the head of the bed—the way any

primate grabs a limb to steady itself—
and there they are again, in my head,

near the end of their fight: the tiger,
and the once-frisky young bull on

that dusty arena floor years ago
in Guilin, China...all the people

yelling, the bull—no longer able to
elude the inexorable claws and teeth,

and gradually winding down—the tiger—
aiming its precise bites again and again

at the same raw spot on the right
foreleg—easily ducking the sluggish,

predictable horns—the bull finally
breaking down, collapsing...the scene

plays out until something gives way in
my mind's merciful dust, loosening

my grip on the bar, yielding to
the softer claws of sleep.

Sparrows In December

Just outside our kitchen window,
about a dozen fluttering opportunists
contend for the four perches
on the feeder, the losers
landing in a nearby bush.

Fidgety, wary, glancing up,
down, sideways, any agitation
(a fork dropped on the countertop)
will turn all of them into a sudden
flock fleeing the snowy yard...

only to return ten minutes later—
a multi-winged, multi-eyed
airborne dynamo until it dissolves
once again into separate
contenders for a feeder perch...

one flutters up from the bush,
flicks off with its wings a smaller
bird, takes its place—pecks a few
times at the seeds then flits away;
another bird flicks a bigger one
only to be quickly chased off
by another...

a minute later, something
(quiet as a sunrise or loud as
a shadow on the snow) starts
the flock sideways through the yard
then skyward over the snowy roofs,
and pine tops and still rising....

Maya

—for Kari

Before Maya, I never knew
a dog could love a human being.

Whenever you were home,
she was close by, often
lying down, the whites
of her eyes showing—her ears
and nose incredibly alert.

She loved the rest of us too.
When we'd visit from
a thousand miles away,
we'd get out of the car and Maya
would be there to meet us,
walking on two legs like all of us,
wrapping her front legs around us
and giving us a hug, her huge tail
wagging frantically.

Maya, Maya, Maya, Maya, Maya
I'd say to her cheerfully,
and I'd have to pry her happiness
off of me, one paw, then the other.

Maya never could contain her joy,
or her sadness, whenever you
left the house: she'd lie there,
close to the door and facing it—
like the needle in a compass
pointing always north—the whites
of her sad eyes showing, waiting...

waiting—for the sequence she
must've loved: first the sound
of your car; then the garage door
opening; then the kitchen door knob
turning...then, like magic,
there you were, with groceries or
one of the kids in your arms,
and Maya's tail would be wagging
joyously, and her claws clicking
frantically on the tiled kitchen floor.

*　　*　　*

One night in October, she wanted you
to open the door for her once more,
and she went out into the backyard
once more. She lay down among
the leaves. I can see her there,
for a few moments, the whites
of her eyes showing, looking
up at a window, wondering
where you were.
And then she died.

*　　*　　*

There are good lives and there are
also good deaths. Sometimes we can
be lucky enough to have had both.

Good dog, Maya.

Cancun, Mexico

A young woman who has paid to swim
with dolphins is lying on her stomach
in the long pool, legs and arms extended,
as two of them surface, exactly together
near her feet, each placing its bottle nose on
an instep arch, and power her at dolphin-speed
across the pool until the trainer's piercing whistle
stops them, and they dive, exactly together,
out of sight, leaving her—after a great whoosh
of waves—standing there and smiling up at
the restaurant crowd, as if she feels like
she's gotten her money's worth.

The pool lights dim and we get up to leave,
as the smallest dolphin is still trying to breach
the glass barricade, I suppose to get to its mother
down at the far end. We stand there a few minutes
watching a turbulent underwater shadow of absolute
hope, pressing its long nose hard against the hard
glass, sliding along it back and forth for twenty
or thirty feet before it disappears.

The Ascent Of Squirrels

This morning after breakfast,
on the sun porch with the morning paper
and coffee with Jan, we watched,
as usual, a squirrel in the ash just outside
our windows, chewing on a fresh
ear of corn I'd stuck on the feeder spike.
I waved once at him, slowly,
and sensing movement, he dropped
the kernel trapped between his paws
and looked up, not at me, but (it seemed)
at the best branch possible for escaping
in his preferred direction: up.

But since my gesture was slow
and benign, he went back to
chewing. Then I waved the sports
section twice, slowly, and up
went his head again, quicker this time,
his tail started flicking, and he leaned
away from the threat, poised to
leap; but again, since the waving
had been brief and the bigger moving
thing not close enough to get too excited
about, he went back to chewing.

Then I thought of Darwin,
and wondered how many millions
of head-raising responses over how

many thousands of generations
it took for that one habit to become
fixed in the brains of squirrel off-spring.

Sipping on my decaf, I could see myself
as an early human with primordial
poetic leanings. I looked at Jan
and couldn't help saying, and smiling
(as if I was the first ever to utter the words):
look before you leap. And she smiled back.

WINTER DYAD

(Watching "Animal Planet")

In high definition,
somewhere in the snows
of the North, a deer
has fallen on a frozen
lake and lies on
its side, spent from
its struggle to stand up.

A helicopter—with
a photographer
inside its glass
brain case—drops
a few hundred feet
for close-ups,
the blades' alien
wind powdering in
the deer's fur,
making it thrash
wildly...
it must feel itself
moving, pushed by
an airborne predator...

the helicopter
turns and retreats...
swings around,
approaches again,
this time closer,
shoving the deer,
inadvertently, into
an opening in the ice...

retreats once more,
the clattering wind
diminishing...

barely moving
in the numbing water,
yet holding its head
erect, the deer
clambers up
onto the ice
on feet not meant
for ice, then falls
just as the helicopter,
with precision timing,
sweeps down
and pushes again,
steering the deer
with its wind—
as if machine
and animal were
tethered to each other
by an invisible, rigid
cable—and just as
they're about to reach
land the one
lifts, stops in the
air, and waits
above the shoreline,
leaving the other
in a heap, but with
a front hoof
touching land.

Darwinian

"Origin of man now proved. He who understands baboon
would do more towards metaphysics than Locke."
        —Charles Darwin, "The M Notebook," 1856

As with our closest kin, the chimpanzees,
      but also baboons, wolverines, and catfish,
      we spend our days mainly looking out for
      number one.

And yet we're not exactly in the habit of admitting
      we're selfish. We've all heard of the football star
      who insists that every touchdown he makes
      is for his team and not himself.

We like to think we are an *unanimal*—
      look at us, we say: *we can think!* (but so can crows);
      or, *we can even think about thinking!*
      (but so can rats).

As in Vervet monkeys,
      girls like to play with dolls, and boys like to monkey
      around with toy trucks. Men prefer women with an 0.7
      hip-to-waist ratio, and women will generally pick
      a dad over a cad.

Regarding forgiveness:
      Johathan Swift said it well: "A brave man thinks no one
      his superior who does him an injury, for he has it then
      in his power to make himself superior to the other,
      by forgiving it."

Regarding status:
> at work, we keep track of who is on which rung of
> the ladder on the way to the top, who goes out for a beer
> with the boss after hours, who has the newest SUV,
> or the house with the most square feet and bathrooms.

Sixty Years Later I Notice,
Inside A Flock Of Blackbirds,

the Venetian blinds
I dusted off

for my mother on
Saturday mornings,

closing, opening them
with the pull cord a few

times just to watch the outside
universe keep blinking,

as the flock suddenly
rises from November stubble,

hovers a few seconds,
closing, opening,

blinking, before it tilts,
then vanishes over a hill.

Protean

"[One way]...of throwing a predator into a tizzy is to behave
in a bizarre, erratic, or seemingly random manner. ... This
strategy was used by submarine commanders during World
War II who tried to confuse the enemy by sailing a random
course determined by throwing dice."
>   —David Livingstone Smith, *Why We Lie*

running—pursued by howling hounds
followed by sweaty horses carrying hunters
dressed in red   the fox is running every which

way   slipping through   wild
  rye   switch grass   white spruce,
       milkweed   sumac
    in and   out of muddy
    ravines (loving the shadows   not
minding the mud)
    poker-faced (his exact
      expression when tensely
        crouched among
      explosions of   feathers   in
      chicken sheds),
      never (if it can help it) surrendering
        as much as a   glint
of or a
          fleck
  of
     red

to any open eye   trying
   every trick he knows (and
      inventing new
            ones on the run)—all this
to quell the hellish howling behind
   his straight-out, white-
                              tipped

      tail....

Encounter On The Sioux River Trail
(July 26, 2010)

Forty yards beyond my bike's
goose neck a real Canadian
honker sees me coming
yet refuses to drop off the
narrow trail into the water
with the others, and I've built
up too much momentum
against a south wind by now
to want to slow down, or
stop and wait for its attitude
to change—or to have to
admit I chickened out...

twenty yards away I *ding*
ding ding ding my bell hard
making the goose stand taller,
expand its wings, avert its
look sideways but keep me
in its sight, and open its beak...

at full speed to divert it I fake
a move toward the river bank
then turn abruptly back—it's
not fooled—and duck as I scoot
past its lofty head, a deep, loud
reptilian hiss raising the hair
on the back of my neck while
wiring itself into my brain
for a long time ahead.

Wounded

("Shark Week" on the Discovery Channel)

A seal barely floating,
with a red gaping gash
on its side, is plucked
from the sea by three men
in an observation boat.
One of them holds it by
the tail as it tries to fling its
head around and bite him,
as the boat cuts the waves
toward an island of seals.
Released close to shore,
this one will survive,
the narrator says, thanks to
a thick layer of fat.

It can happen that way:
one day something suddenly
hits you from below, flings
you high in the air and upside
down, you land with a hard
alien smack, flail around
a few minutes, discover
you're barely upright.

Somehow, you reach a safe
place without being hit again,
and then you do the only thing
you can do: lie there and suffer

until you're strong enough and
hungry enough to venture out—
but from now on and for a long
time, with your eyes open wider,
your moves lighter and quicker,
if not quite as deep and far out
as before that first hit and that
first red wound.

At The Mammoth Dig In Hot Springs, South Dakota

walking on a ramp rising higher and higher,
station to station through the huge,
vaulted, wooden enclosure over
an ancient sink hole—the beams
dense and sturdy enough for Noah's Ark—
we listen, with earphones, to the voice
of an older woman informing us
about the exposed, hard, cold remains
of creatures dead 24,000 years:

massive skeletal heads, broken-off tusks;
an upper torso deprived of a head;
teeth, clavicles, femurs; one completely
intact, curving backbone...

about ten feet beneath the highest, final
station, a pretty female student
in a white, low-cut blouse—more
than a hint of cleavage showing—
and two male students are sitting
on the yellowish, meticulously
worked-on prehistoric ground—
each with a fine brush, leaning
slightly forward, head down,
brushing dust.

Farm Scene Synesthesia

"...darker than the inside of a cow."
                              —Mark Twain

Speaking of darkness, of cows,
take the word **cattle**. To me, that short "a"
sound—in fact, in any word—always
looks and sounds black, or at least dark.
Which is why I've always enjoyed the delicious
redundancy of the phrase, **black angus**.

Imagine a herd of white-faced black angus
standing near a grain bin on a warm summer day.
Speaking of words and the things
they name, now add the word **shadow**,
the bin's, that is, juxtaposing it with **cattle**.
They even rime, they fit so well together.

And now add one more word that fits well
with **shadow** and **cattle: grass**. There
they are, grazing in the shadowed grass,
two of them with raised faces, looking
beyond toward green, wide fields
in the bright West River sunlight.

TWO

The Writer

Some mornings as a boy—my father away
at work—I'd be standing there alone
in the basement, listening to the whitewashed
silence, watching the fresh morning light
brightening the high, undersized windows...

always I'd head for his beat-up desk in the corner
near the clotheslines, and if sheets were hanging
brush my cheek lightly against them and smell
their freshness on the way...

I'd sit in his creaky wooden chair, the way
he did, and swivel around on steel rollers
biting the cracked concrete. I'd sit up tall
and face the Underwood, pick at the keys
his way (two-finger-style), cock an eye
the way he did—at my own imagined words
on my own imagined sheet of paper.

What Comes Back

"David Evans, 4-year-old son of Mr. and Mrs. Arthur C. Evans,
narrowly escaped drowning when he was swept from his feet
and carried through a culvert by a flashflood at 35th and
Lafayette. Quick action on the part of Allen Jimison, 28,
and his dog Boots, saved the lad's life. ... The voice of the
boy's mother was virtually lost temporarily as she screamed
for help when she saw him swept away."
    —from *The Sioux City Journal*, June 7, 1944

Reading each fading word again, I'd think that
something, some detail or image of being swept from
my feet and carried through that tunnel of muddy
darkness would come back—but not so. And nothing
comes back of Jimison either, standing there (I learned
years later) working his frantic shovel at the far end
of the culvert; or his dog he'd sent in after me to
help clear a breathless path through a tangle of
corn stalks and branches.

    And yet what does come back is as fresh
in my mind as this morning's newsprint: standing on
the mud-slicked bank above the ditch, refusing to look
down or let go of a barbed-wire fence—a man's huge,
hairy hands gripping mine, prying my fingers loose,
one by one...shivering in a bathtub, my teeth chattering,
my mother washing my back with a warm washrag...
wrapping me in a towel after helping me over the
slippery edge of cold porcelain...her voice being lost,
no words come back—but her busy hands do,
and her urgent, hazel eyes.

Mortal Leaps

Back in the '40s, often on breaks
in the inky pressroom under
the quaking sidewalk, the young pressmen,
including my father, would leap
against a wall to see who could leave
the highest marks with inky fingertips.

I picture them crouched like cats,
then springing from the greasy floor
in their black steel-toed shoes
and bib overalls and paper caps
made out of yesterday's news, some
caps flying off with their grunting efforts.
Up, up they went, over and over,
touching higher and higher.

I forgot who told me that my father's
marks were a record for years.
Maybe he was the one. After all,
according to a long-retired fellow
pressman I talked to, decades after
his death, he liked to tell others about
his habit of reading three or four books
at a time and remembering what every
one of them said, and if anybody
wanted quotes for proof, he had plenty
of them on the tip of his tongue.

To me, well into middle age, my father's
ink-stained marks were up there with
those made by a Mikan or a Chamberlain.

But time being the great leveler,
in recent years the so-called record

has dropped a few inches out of
my mind's realm of the mythical.
Whenever I drive by the place in Sioux City
where the *Journal* building used to be—
it was razed decades ago and replaced by
a two-story parking lot—all that noise
and quaking under the sidewalk comes
back to me, along with memories
of the leapers, all dead, including my father.

Now 69, I too am leaping up to put down
these words in ink—in honor, as a cherished
and cherishing son, an exaggerator,
a lover of books, a quoter, a man no more
and no less mortal than my father.

Magic

It's about time I said this
(my mother gone 30 years):
not quite all of the sting has gone out of
that after-midnight scene in our house
on the railroad bluff over half a century ago.

It started with a stubborn defiance
of curfew one too many nights,
and then my being sure that I could slip
in as quietly as a burglar. And yet I
didn't expect to see the rough lath
in her hand as she stood just inside
the kitchen door—or the fury in her eyes.

It's magical, the way some wounds—
on thighs, on knees or in the heart—
can keep on stinging for so many years,
and yet even as they're stinging,
healing with forgiveness.

The Greatest

Whenever I hear Pavarotti sing, I think of my father,
dead nearly 50 years. I can still see him,

stretched out on his long, naugahyde
recliner—his big feet with black nylon socks

sticking out over the end, his eyes closed—
listening to Caruso, Lanza, or Jan Pierce

on his portable Sears record player, after his eight
hours in the loud, inky pressroom. I can still see

his shy yet confident smile and hear his words:
"Caruso was the greatest " (even if that sweet

voice from so long ago was so scratchy on the old
recordings). I wish I could bring my father back

in the new century, along with his recliner,
and play for him a perfectly clear recording

of Pavarotti. What would he think? My good
guess is that when listening to Pavarotti he'd be

thinking of Caruso, and I can hear him saying,
when the arias were finished—especially his

favorite, from Aida—that he loved that voice,
but that Caruso was still the greatest. No doubt,

hearing his words I'd do the same thing today
that I did at 14—smile and nod my head.

Weekend Bowling League

This morning at breakfast,
eating cold cereal and reading
the sports pages, I heard
the sudden thunder
of bowling pins in a TV ad

and was back at War Eagle Lanes,
downtown under the sidewalks
in my early teens.
My father, in his dark green
bowling shirt announcing
The Sioux City Journal, front
and back, had just thrown
his seventh straight strike,
and was wandering around
(as usual, when he was on
a hot streak), talking to other
bowlers on other lanes,
too nervous to sit down
and wait for his turn.

Then he came over to the bench
my mother and I were sitting on.
I could tell by his eyes he was
happy, and he had to know
(the way I always followed him
around with my eyes) that I was
happy too. He came up to me,
put an arm on my shoulder, bent
over and kissed me on the cheek.

I turned a page of the sports,
and when I put my hand to my face
it wasn't my own but my father's
scratchy whiskers that I had felt
55 years ago.

On An Old Black And White Photograph

As if you'd agreed, at 15, grudgingly, to give up a few
precious seconds of sprinting and soaring already
half way through the '50s, to just stand there—
in dark gym trunks and white, smudged, Converse
tennis shoes, your brand-new, blonde flat-top shining
in summer sunlight—gripping, near your right hip
with both hands, the taped end of a bamboo vaulting pole.
You're smiling a cocky smile for the camera, held by
Jerry Nyreen, your friend with the black, wild hair.
Could you or Jerry have guessed, just before the click,
that he'd have no choice but to make you—the one
who taught him—the second best Icarus on the block?
Your pole is aimed straight down a packed-dirt runway
toward a pit dug up with a spade and full of lumber-yard
sawdust, in a vacant lot, on a railroad bluff overlooking
the Burlington Northern trains on tracks aimed for places
with mythical names like Chicago, Minneapolis, Omaha.

1957—The Two Of Us

1. At Crystal Lake

Waking up in the heat of mid-August in the back seat
of my parents' '54 Chevy in a panic a few minutes from

midnight—our curfew was 10—starting up the car and
spinning the wheels, jerking back and forth from drive to

reverse, going nowhere again except deeper into the sand
because I'd parked too close to the smooth, moonlit water...

scrambling down the beach toward the lantern and the huge guy
in a lumber jack shirt (a beef lugger at Armour's, I was thinking)

sitting on an overturned bucket, sipping on a bottle of beer,
fishing for bullheads, a few swishing around in a nearby bucket...

he nodding when I asked could he *please* help us with our car
down the beach that's stuck way past curfew, you adding

one more *please*... a few minutes later the two of us sitting
in the car, watching the huge man trudging toward us, my hands

already gripping the wheel, wishing he'd speed it up but he,
apparently, not a man to be rushed... then, leaning on one

Paul Bunyan hand on the top of the rolled-down window, telling me
to just go easy and steady on the gas and steer gradually toward

dry land and we'd be okay... me imagining him putting his
beef lugger's shoulder to the back bumper, feeling the car

moving steadily under his power... then, out of the sand and
rolling free, turning my head and yelling back *thank you! thank*

you man! and he not even looking up and yet his raised hand saying to us *you're welcome* or *just keep going* or both...

getting back to Leeds, letting you out at your house across
the alley, burning around the corner, seeing the light on in

the kitchen, turning the headlights off just before turning into
the driveway, parking quietly... opening the kitchen

door right into my mother's severe frown and expected
news: no car for me for the rest of the month, period...

waking up Sunday morning, opening the blinds to the
bright new sun, knowing the two of us were forgiven and

safe, for now, feeling more in love than ever, with plenty
of summer left before the start of our senior year.

2. In the Dark

It was on a weekend and well past midnight,
my parents asleep, and the two of us
were entangled on the floor...

(not that we hadn't been warned sternly
regarding our teenage passion.
My mother to me, over an ironing board:
"You know what's gonna happen if
you two keep on like this."
Your mother to you, as she was stirring
something in a pan on the stove:
"if you play with fire, you'll get burned."

...we were on the round, braided rug,
as usual, but with one huge thrill of a difference:
our clothes were in careless piles too far
from our entanglement to be reached.
Then we heard the bedroom door open and

froze. I looked up, could barely make out the tall,
daunting shape of my father filling the hallway
entrance—his profile said he wasn't looking
our way, but just standing there, having sensed,
I was sure, our presence. Paralyzed,
we waited for a light to go on. It didn't.
Then the shape was gone.

*   *   *

Now, 54 years later, sipping a beer together on
our sun porch before dinner, as usual, we sometimes
recall the scene, laughing at our terror, our
helplessness, agreeing once again that, even if
the light had gone on, it wouldn't finally have made
(as my father would say) one iota of a difference.

Youth (Summer, 1956)

"The season of youth is brief."
    —Pindar

HERE COMES KEMP
said the tall sign on the roof
of the rumbling wrecker truck—

we paused, watching—
Eddie at shortstop, twirling his glove
on his wiry wrist, me the catcher,
standing up, my hand raised
to stop the pitch—

we turned, watched the truck go by:
THERE GOES KEMP
said the sign.

Idling In My '86 Ford Festiva At A Red Light In Rapid City,
After The Sturgis Motorcycle Rally 25 Years Ago

That's how I left them there...

he, beer-bellied, in his 50s,
helmeted, straddling his
upright, bigger and shinier
Harley slanted toward
the curb, in black leather
pants and white T-shirt,
coaxing, pleading with
his girlfriend, yet trying
not to make a scene—
"come on, come on"—
to get back on his bike...

she, much younger—
one arm completely
missing—standing on
the sidewalk, her helmet
dangling at her hip,
slim and shapely,
in matching leather and
T-shirt, long blonde hair,
her face flushed, fierce
and tear-stained...

when the light turned green.

THREE

You have got hold of the wrong absolutes and infinities.
God as absolute? God as infinity? I don't even understand the words.
I'll tell you what is absolute and infinite. Loving a woman.

—Walker Percy

Seven P.M., February 13, 2006

You are right now in the air
on the way to Denver, as I

type these words in the basement.
You, who reminded me,

before we left for the airport,
where the key is to the

strong box on a closet shelf.
You, who stood there at

the airport check-in desk,
your perfect hair matching

your brown suede jacket,
holding your two carry-on bags—

one with a new book,
and a crossword puzzle that

you always get busy on during
take off. Starting today,

I'll mope around,
teach my classes, read a little,

and write something for you
each day you're gone.

Dyadic

Your absence makes
the house grow quieter.

So sitting here at my desk,
with its twin pull-out boards—

the left one for coffee, the right one
for beer (after 5 P.M.)—

I can hear better, and except for
the hum of my computer—

I notice that everything is in pairs:
on my left, a wall clock ticking;

on my right, a wall clock ticking;
in back of me, drops of water falling

into two hanging buckets from
a couple of leaky sprinkler valves.

I double check the time: 5:08, 5:09.
You know what that means:

I get up and walk past my two
dictionaries, the basement bed,

to the basement fridge and pull out
the first of two cold Budweisers.

Not Unlike A Convict

I X out each day you're gone,
on my calendar.

Talking In Bed

Now I've got somebody else
to talk to in bed. Myself.

I mention the job,
the weather, the widening crack

in the driveway. All I can
think of to say back is

I know, I know, I know.
When I think of turning

over, you're not there to turn
over with. So I say anyway,

out of habit, quietly, to myself:
Let's turn over. And I do.

Ten Things I Don't Mind About Sleeping Alone

I can go to bed at 9 o'clock.
I can sprawl—use the whole bed if I want to,
   and not have to sleep so close to the edge
   that my arm hangs out in the cold air.
I can hook a foot over the bottom
   of the bed, when I'm on my stomach.
I can use all four pillows, even your silk one,
   that never warms up like the others.
I can have total control of the remote control.
I can surf as much as I want to, and skip the commercials.
I can watch boxing or ultimate fighting.
I can use all the blankets, even the bed spread, if I get cold.
I can sleep on my back.
I can get up in the morning and not
   have to make the bed.

On The Sixth Morning

I get into the car, turn the key
and get only a dull click.
So I go back inside, pick up the phone
to call Triple A., but when I push the
on button, I get nothing again,
because last night after we talked
on the new phone, I put it back on
the receiver face down instead of face up.

I go upstairs, call Triple A on my cell phone,
eat some oatmeal, read the paper.
And then I remember your urgent note
about watering the flowers on Saturday.
I fill up the plastic pitcher, take it to
the TV room, and pour so much water
on the flowers on top of the CD player
that it spills into the guts of the machine!
I sprint to the kitchen for a towel,
sprint back and wipe off what I can get,
but I figure the machine is shot.
(Remember the boom box we took
to China, that blew up when I
plugged it into our Chinese outlet?)

The man from Triple A comes out
and jumps the battery, but says we might
need a new alternator. After he leaves,
I need to deal with some nervous
energy so I drive to the gym and
climb 62 steps, three times in a row.

Feeling better, I go home and put some
Chinese folk music on the CD player,
which has had time to dry out by now—
fumble with the knobs a little, and—
it works!

So now, my missed love,
I'm ready to start my day.

The Arrival

Driving home today from Walmart—
since we'll be moving soon from
this town we've lived in for
39 years, I didn't go straight home
but circled some blocks,
passing a couple of our old houses,
and the kids' grade school.
I imagined them chasing balls in
the playground, with nothing else
on their mind but chasing balls in
the playground—they were that
small. And I thought of how
our several moves in town have
been more and more southward,
in the direction of the first town
we lived in after we got married—
the one, in fact, we'll be moving
back to in a few months. Then
I thought of some lines by
T.S. Eliot, that *the end of our*
exploration must be to arrive
Where we started, and know the place
for the first time, worth saying
aloud to myself through a windshield.

Sometime Soon

...come downstairs in
that purple robe,
and we'll have some
serious fun

Vice Versa

It's true:
You don't like

everybody I like,
and vice versa.

And yet—
I love you

and vice versa.
Leave it at that?

And yet, and yet—
I'll leave it at that—

and vice versa?

Do Not Disturb

How to sum up
51 years together?

You said it best in your
China journal—
April 14, 1993:

"After a lunch of tea eggs,
peanut butter crackers and fruit,
we hung the 'Do Not Disturb'
sign out on our door and had
a nice, relaxing nap, swaying to
the rhythm of the boat as it
made its way up the Yangtze."

FOUR

Lilies

"Consider the lilies of the field, how they grow;
they toil not, neither do they spin. And yet I say
unto you, that Solomon in all his glory was not
arrayed like one of these."
                    —Luke 12:27

For instance, our first one to open up
this spring—this morning I held it,
and looked inside. A rare thing for me.
Six years into a restless retirement,
it's as if I still need to spend my days
earning a paycheck.
                    But what if, by day's
end, all I can say I accomplished was
that I bent down and held the silken
petals of a yellow lily, and looked deep
inside its soft, upturned bell? Just that
for a whole day's earnings?

The Details

even 60 years back
are still sharp-edged

as the small chunks
of salt (from my father's

second job,
on the loading dock

at Armour's) in my hand
after reaching

deep into a pocket
of his tall Bib overalls

hanging on a nail
at the top of the basement

steps—the crimp
in a pant leg,

the thin shoulder straps,
the silver buttons,

even the grainy taste
of salt on my tongue.

At The Health Club

1. Eye to Eye

At 82 and terribly hunched over,
he pushes his walker slowly, shakily

around the track...and often singles
me out because I listen, and because

I'm sitting at the biceps or triceps
machine, which means that when he

halts a few feet away, and leans over
his walker toward me—steadying

himself with trembling hands—
his face, unlike a child's, can be

level with another man's...he often
mentions his wife, with heart failure;

how he's tried to talk her into
coming to the club for exercise,

but who always says she's had
her fill of exercise for one lifetime;

and then he tells me—his face
brightening—how good it makes

him feel whenever he comes here,
even if it's only a couple days

a week...slowly, shakily, he heads
back to the track, having found

at least one man who agrees with him
that coming here is worth the time

and the effort, and whom he can
speak to eye to eye.

2. *Middle-Aged Man in a Wheelchair Shooting Baskets*

He prefers to be alone on the court
so he can wheel freely between both

baskets—when he misses a shot and
the ball *clangs* off the backboard,

bounces a few times and rolls away
toward the opposite end, he's after it

with dogged speed—as if he's playing
for keeps in a real game and all the other

players in wheelchairs are invisible...
at first you wonder how he'll pick up

the loose ball when he gets to it, since
he can't bend far enough forward to

grab it with both hands, but it's easy:
he rolls up alongside the ball, slows

slightly, then reaches (he's a lefty) over
his left wheel, traps it niftily against the

shielded spokes and—as if looking
around for someone to pass to—scoops

it up and over and into his lap, steering
with his right hand on the other wheel,

then keeps on wheeling to his special spot—
a foot behind the free throw line—slows

again, stops, sets himself, facing the basket
with dogged, eager focus, and lets fly—

I've seen him make four in a row, nothing
but net...the chest of the white T-shirt

he wears most days says in bold green letters:
IT TAKES WORK TO BE CHAMPION.

   3. *Obsessions: An Indoor Journey*

I'm pumping on my favorite
bike and celebrating (in a song

under my breath) new capillaries
sprouting near my replenished

heart, and a thin woman in
her 20s (a regular like me)

walks by, clasping to her chest—
as if it's more vital than usual—

a thick book, making me lift
myself and lean forward

a little to both ease my vitals
and get a peek at the title,

as she steps up on her favorite
treadmill and lays open,

like the wings of a gigantic
preserved butterfly, her book

before a pair of pretty eyes
and a red bandana—

making me wonder if she's
simply committed herself

to reading *The Road to Hell,*
or committed herself to

the road to hell,
period.

Gymnast In Serious Condition After Fall
—newspaper headline

God saw it all and didn't lift a finger.
The next morning, He had two surgeons
insert a metal plate and two steel rods
into the bone in her beautiful back.
Whispering into her ear during surgery,
He thought it best to let her know the severity
of her injury, and what to say to her parents
when she woke up: *Everything happens*
for a reason. And then He gave her more
words to give as a gift to friends who came to
her hospital room: *He will take care of it,*
and I will win.

Without lifting a finger, He made her feet
forget how to stay on the balance beam,
and her hips how to clear the uneven
bars and the horse. But everything above
the waist He left alone. That way, her hands
could finally heal—no more bloody calluses,
or bandages, or chalk for a sure grip. And her
elbows, her shoulders, her face, her blonde hair,
her beautiful smile—all would be taken care of,
so she could win.

Something Our Ancient Ancestors
Didn't Prepare Us For

Every one of the 747's wheels has to touch
concrete before the nervous ones like me can say
to themselves, *a little rough but I'm still here...*
but then we're being hurled across the tarmac so fast
in this huge, cigar-shaped vibrating contraption
that I expect it to shake apart any second...
and now, slowing down, most of my fellow passengers
might agree with me that this won't be our last
flight after all...so then it's time to swallow and gape
to unclog the ears, and just before coming to a complete
stop (even though the seat belt signs are still on) all
around us we hear the impatient, lucky, comforting
click, click, click of seat belts, unloosening...

In The Minneapolis-St. Paul Airport

I'm walking to my gate, brooding
on dark yesterdays and darker

tomorrows, when a title in a bookstore
window stops me. I buy the book.

Nearby, in a chair at my gate, I close
my eyes and speak the words of

the title under my breath, slowly,
over and over: *The Power of Now.*

When I open my eyes and look up,
a well-dressed, attractive woman

about 40 is walking by, as if in no
hurry, inspecting her surroundings

so intently, it's as if she's cleared
her mind of everything except

what she's looking at: *now,*
a flight attendant pausing to

adjust her purse strap; *now,* a boy
about 10, his legs dangling from

the edge of his seat, awkwardly
working a red yoyo...for another

breathing moment I watch her—
see her step with grace, like

a ballerina, onto a moving walkway,
then stop walking yet keep on

moving with others ahead and
behind her until she disappears

from my sight into the future
and the past.

Primal Winter

What cave man, scraping rocks and bones
for a million years, would've heard
anything like the sound—on a cold
December morning—of scraping
a pickup's ice-crusted windshield?

He gets in and looks out and sees he's
skimped again: the holes are the size
of a pair of pre-adolescent heads—
yet he drives off anyway (it's getting late),
one-handed, steam rising from his coffee
mug in the warm grip of his left glove,
leaning forward as far as he can, his jaw
nearly touching the steering wheel—reading
the streets the way a scholar reads a rare
text in a university archives.

Just after passing the freeway sign he opens
his side windows for better vision and is
hit by a blast of Pleistocene wind on his
neck, and all he can do now is hope
that the gradually-growing heads he's
peering through—with help from the defrost
and the wipers on high speed—will be big
enough by the time he must merge with
the freeway's primitive, mad traffic.

Watching Bull Riders

there's one moment I can appreciate:
just after the eight-second buzzer
goes off, and the man–who has stayed
on top of the wide, hard back
of a hyped-up beast for a successful ride–
now must figure out a way to get off
without being kicked or stomped on,
so he loosens his deep grip
and begins to lean to one side
of the animal, trusting it'll sense that he's
falling off and will go ahead and shake him
loose in the same direction he's leaning–
which means that the rider (whether or not
the bull knows it) is able to exert at least
a modicum of choice as to where
and how he's about to land.

Whenever I see this, I understand better
about trusting myself under some duress
to do what's right: about leaning into a fear,
allowing it to take me where it will,
even if I end up–successful ride or not–
with my face and teeth clogged with dirt,
and a sore back, or knee.

Keeping The Balance

"Find something in your life to be good at,"
my father used to say back in that
decade-in-deadly-earnest, the '50s—
and here it is, well over half a century later,
and I'm still stuck under the thumb
of his admonition.

I like to watch that greyhound-thin fellow
in our town who rides his unicycle
to work every day except in rain or snow.
I've even seen him pumping a small
dumbbell in one hand as he's pumping
vigorously up the fairly steep hill
behind the high school.

Recently, not long after my 70th birthday,
I thought up a new endeavor of my own:
Every day I make sure to always put on
my socks—at home, or after a shower
at the club—by balancing on one leg
at a time, completely free of any support.

My father was not easily impressed,
so I don't know if my modest endeavor
would qualify, in his eyes—though I think
the unicycle riding would—as something
to be good at. But it doesn't matter.
It works for me. Though I'm far from
perfect—I sometimes lose my balance
and have to start over, but usually
it takes just a slight hop or two to stay

upright. And I'm a lot better now
than when I started.

2.

A coin Jan and I bought many years ago
on The Isle of Man, just off England
in the Irish Sea—gulls screamed
into the wind as they followed our ferry
northward—shows three lithe acrobat legs
connected to one another, in a circle—
which means, if you fall, you'll always
land upright, on one sure foot (or, as we
see it, at least not break a leg or hip).

So far for us, so good.
May you too be lucky.

Cartoon Universals

1. *Thinking Can Be Harmful to Your Health*

Imagine the scene: you are literally way out on a limb
and your enemy is busy sawing

it off (or maybe you're the one doing
the sawing). Whatever you do, don't look

down. But of course you do, abruptly
ending the scene with your fall.

2. *Luck and Muscles*

You're a guy in a sailor cap with a pipe,
a gravelly, alpha voice, and super-sized forearms—

you're at a construction site just after being
cold cocked by the Paul Bunyan-sized fist of

another alpha male (in your ongoing arms
race over an hour-glass-shaped, black-haired girl

with a tedious voice), and you're walking—still
out cold—on a steadily-rising steel girder many

giddy floors up, and just as you reach the end of it
and are about to step off into oblivion, another

girder, ideally timed, meets your foot so all you do is
keep on walking and rising until, stepping off, another

girder replaces the last one so you continue walking,
now 50 or so floors up, and your power source—

a can of spinach in your shirt pocket—begins to
bulge like your biceps, the sea fog clears in your head

(your testosterone level rising like crane-lifted girders),
and then in the final scene with a final *blamb* of

your famous fist you win back the girl for a night
on the town, or better yet, marriage, and a family.

   3. *The Triumph of the Inconspicuous*

You're a remarkably resourceful coyote
that'll do anything to catch a nondescript

beeping road runner with infinite speed
and plenty of gears, so to catch him you

shoot yourself out of cannons, zoom
across the prairie on jet skates,

mail yourself in a package marked:
"Road Runner"...and still, after all

your ingenious, hard work you're
nothing more than a loser. Meanwhile,

your boring, putative prey is effortlessly
speeding far, far away, *beep beep*.

   4. *In This World, You Never Die*

You're a cat that's been flattened
into its shadow by a mouse with an

outrageously oversized sledge hammer;
no problem: you're up in a jiffy on all

four paws and feeling fine in the next
scene, once again skittering mouse-

ward, spitting out your fate, while
your tiny enemy, now a furred

blurr...now hiding behind a wall,
is holding the hugest sledge hammer

in history—it's poised and waiting
for you, portending stars.

July: Nightly News In The Heartland

All I can think about is
my cattle.

Four missing,
rustlers suspected—
all day driving around
in his pickup looking for
his cattle...

a man can't afford
to lose that much money.

Seed hat tipped up...

I can't even sleep
at night.

Rubbing his eyes
with his fists...

all I can think about is
my cattle.

At The Empire Mall

Your wife's been gone now for a decade
from lung cancer, you're 84 and alone—
what better way to burn a few hours of
a cold winter morning than to show up
at the mall at seven sharp, when the doors
open for the mall walkers? Soon you're
tottering down the Penney's hall on your cane
and a bad left knee, then veering left into
the Food Court, to occupy your accustomed table
and chair. You lean your cane, drape your yellow
coat over a chair back, ready for your main
daily MO: to waylay, if you can, two or three
walkers for a few minutes to shoot the breeze.

You watch the sober, quiet, indoor parade go by:
the quick-stepping, pretty young woman
in grey tights, her key ring jingling in one hand
on every other step; some heavy couples
in their 50s who come to shed some pounds,
some women gripping tiny barbells; a retired
couple with a serious look aimed straight ahead,
their day already organized (shopping at HyVee
in the morning, exchanging an oversized picture
frame at Walmart in the afternoon); an older
ex-runner in a purple jogging suit who looks
like he's doing the Empire Mall Indoor 10-K.

All go past you on their laps, some cutting
corners and skipping halls, others in earnest who
take every hall (even the one to the restrooms)
to the very end, rounding a planter the way
a rodeo girl rounds a barrel on her horse.

But still, most mornings at least a couple of
retired guys with no great plans for the day
can spare 15 minutes to sit and chat with the old
man with sparkling eyes and a cheerful smile,
who can opine on the economy, the health bill,
Medicare, global warming, taxes, you name it.
The talk is the same as the talk in small-town cafes,
minus the ritual of coffee (the shops open at 10).
Soon after the last guy gets up to go, and the last
walker has come around for the last time, you're up
and tottering on your cane—a little stiff from sitting—
back to the Penney's hall and down to the entrance
and out the door, back in your old Chevy occupying
your accustomed spot, since your wife's been gone.

Turning 70
(Remembering Okoboji, Iowa, 1957)

...*click, click, click, click, click* went the wheels
of our little roller coaster car taking us slowly,
irrevocably upward to the top of the carnival until,
click   click   click—we slowed more, hesitated,
then, cresting out, began to fall, my guts whirling,
my primate grip strangling the safety bar,
my eyes locked shut on what we couldn't help
being headed for straight down—

then, picking up speed, the inevitable *letting go*
because we had no other choice, against a force
huger than carnivals, planets, universes—
so we all opened our eyes and reached as high
as we could for moons, for stars, then came
our avalanching screams.

That's it—exactly what I need to get back to:
that *letting go* (minus the giddy guts), with my eyes
fiercely wide open, each day seconding Prospero's
"be cheerful, sir," and Lao Tzu's tree bending
in the wind, each day looking forward to enjoying
what's left of the ride, the carnival, the life.

David Allan Evans was born in Sioux City, Iowa. He has a BA from Morningside College, an MA from the University of Iowa and an MFA. from the University of Arkansas. He is the author of eight collections of poems, and his writing has received grants from the National Endowment for the Arts and the Bush Artist Foundation of St. Paul, Minnesota. Twice he has been a Fulbright Scholar in China. He was a professor of English at South Dakota State University for 39 years, and Writer-in-Residence. In 2002 he was appointed Poet Laureate of South Dakota. He lives in Sioux Falls with his wife Jan.